The Very Kind

A Surrogacy Story
for Children

MW00955755

Written and illustrated by

Kimberly Kluger-Bell, LMFT

Copyright © 2013 Kimberly Kluger-Bell

All rights reserved.

ISBN 1482621525

ISBN-13 9781482621525

For All the Miracle Children of the World,
Their Courageous Parents,
And Their Gracious Surrogates

I'm a little bear,
But not just any bear,
I'm a koala bear!
And this is my story.

I live in a forest,
And I like to eat leaves
(yum)!

When I was little,
I used to ride on my mommy's back!
We went everywhere together.

Before baby koalas are born,
They usually grow inside
their mommy's pouch ...

Until they get big enough,
To pop their heads up and
come outside!

My mommy and daddy saw lots
of other little koalas around,
And they wanted one too!
But my mommy's pouch couldn't
carry any baby koalas.

This made them very sad but they went to a doctor,
Who said he could help them have the baby they wanted so much!

He knew a
very kind koala
(with babies
of her own),
Who said
she would be
happy to help!

So
the doctor
put the
tiny little
baby bear
that was me,

Into the
kind koala bear's
pouch...

Where I
grew and
grew until

I was big enough,

To pop my head up
and come outside!

And the kind koala gave me back to my mommy and daddy,
And I climbed right up on my mommy's back!

My mommy and daddy wrote a very nice thank you note,
To the very kind koala who carried me in her pouch.

Dear Kind Koala,

Because of your generosity
and kindness our wonderful
baby koala finally was born.
We could not be happier!
Thank you so very much.

All of our love,
The Koala Family

And the very kind koala and her family,
Were very happy to help out!

And we were happy too.
And very, very grateful!

My Story (for you to fill in)

MY NAME _____

WHERE I WAS BORN _____

WHEN I WAS BORN _____

HOW BIG I WAS _____

MY MOMMY'S NAME _____

MY DADDY'S NAME _____

WHERE WE LIVE _____

OUR DOCTOR'S NAME _____

OUR SURROGATE'S NAME _____

WHERE SHE LIVES _____

OTHER THINGS WE KNOW ABOUT HER AND HER FAMILY _____

_____

Me and My Family

Draw a picture here.

Our House

Draw a picture here.

My Surrogate and Her Family

Draw a picture here.

About This Book

In the past several decades, gestational surrogacy has become an increasingly common family-building option. Initially, parents were advised that it was neither necessary nor helpful to tell children about their parents' use of surrogacy. As time has passed, however, it has become increasingly clear that children born to gestational carriers are entitled to know this information about their origins and that this knowledge is not in any way detrimental to parent-child bonds.

The Very Kind Koala is designed to introduce young children to the concept of surrogacy in the animal world. After reading the story, parents can talk to their children about their birth stories—both the medical help that was needed, and the generosity of the surrogate and her family.

All children are miracles, but those carried by surrogate are especially blessed since there were so many more people who helped to bring them into the world. This fact, rather than being something to be hidden, is something that needs to be celebrated.

Made in the USA
Las Vegas, NV
08 December 2021

36586027R00017